Lure the Tiger

Negotiating in confronting circumstances

Lure the Tiger

Negotiating in confronting circumstances

Leonie McKeon

DoctorZed
Publishing
www.doctorzed.com

Books may be ordered through booksellers or by contacting: www.leoniemckeon.com

ISBN: 978-0-6481314-7-2 (hc)
ISBN: 978-0-6481314-6-5 (sc)
ISBN: 978-0-6481314-5-8 (ebk)

A CiP number for this title can be found at the National Library of Australia.

Cover image © Trish Pollock

Printed in Australia, UK and USA.
rev. date 10/04/2019

Contents

Acknowledgements   vi

Leonie's Journey Continues   1

What is Face   5

Strategies for Attack   7

Strategy Thirteen   9

Strategy Fourteen   20

Strategy Fifteen   30

Strategy Sixteen   41

Strategy Seventeen   52

Strategy Eighteen   65

Your Next Steps   78

Acknowledgements

*A*s I conclude this third book in *The Dao of Negotiation: The Path Between Eastern Strategies and Western Minds* I realise how much support I receive from so many people to make the project happen. There are many people involved in creating a book, including my publisher Dr. Scott Zarcinas at DoctorZed Publishing, my editor Hari Teah, and my designer Trish Pollock at BrandArk, all of whom I want to thank. I particularly want to thank Carla Morelli for her excellent research skills, which have made such a positive contribution to *Lure the Tiger: Negotiating in confronting circumstances.* Jennifer McKeon has continued to read and re-read drafts and to provide unlimited faith and belief in me and the project. Finally, I want to thank organisational psychologist Shelley Rogers who has helped me think through the complexities of many of the examples. More importantly, Shelley remains entirely supportive of me and the *The Dao of Negotiation* project, for which I am endlessly appreciative.

"The opportunity of defeating the enemy is provided by the enemy himself."

Sun Tzu, *The Art of War*

Leonie's Journey Continues

After studying Mandarin Chinese for one year in Taiwan my world really opened up. I lived in Taipei in the north, and once my Mandarin was reasonable I moved to the southern city of Kaohsiung. This move really accelerated my Mandarin reading, writing and speaking skills. There were very few Westerners living in Kaohsiung at that time. Without a good understanding of Mandarin it would have been difficult to live there because there was minimal English spoken. Unlike Taipei, in Kaohsiung all of the street signs and many of the everyday signs were in Chinese characters. There was no Pinyin pronunciation system in Taiwan, so the only way to learn to read Mandarin was to learn the Chinese characters. The Pinyin system is explained in Book One – *Tame the Tiger: Negotiating from a position of Power.*

When I first moved to Kaohsiung I had the task of finding my friend and myself an apartment because I could read the Chinese characters, whereas my friend could just speak Mandarin. There was no internet in those days so my task was to search through the Chinese newspaper advertisements for an apartment. My most precious souvenir from Taiwan is my lease, because I had to sign it in Chinese characters, and of course the whole document was written in Chinese characters.

Kaohsiung was the new frontier for foreigners, and employment opportunities were plentiful for those of us who knew how to read, write and speak Mandarin. Many

Chinese people were keen to learn English. During my time in Kaohsiung I worked in both an upmarket adult education English language school, and a popular children's school. I also had a job editing a series of children's English as a Second Language (ESL) books. In this position I was the only Western person working in an office with twenty Chinese people.

At the end of the first year in Kaohsiung we went to Nepal for the Christmas and Chinese New Year break. Nepalese fashion was becoming popular in Taiwan. My entrepreneurial spirit saw a desire in the market and so we started a business importing Nepalese clothing into Kaohsiung. We created business relationships with several tailors in Kathmandu and had Tibetan jackets and dresses made to sell in Kaohsiung.

Kaohsiung has a famous night market called *Liu He Lu*. To sell our imported clothing and accessories we set up a stall there two to three nights a week. This would happen after we finished teaching at the English language school at 10.00pm. We were the only Westerners selling goods on the night market.

This was a place where I saw negotiations taking place constantly between the traders and buyers, and more importantly for me, between the stallholders and the police. In the latter interactions I learnt to just follow what was going on and to do what I was told. If the other stallholders said, "*Mei guanxi*" (no problem), I knew I did not have to worry. A negotiation had taken place, and it was alright for us to stay. But if the stallholders said, "*Pao, pao, pao*" (run,

run, run), I knew we had to pack up and run as fast as we could. Our business, and particularly the arrangement at the market, worked because my Mandarin was good enough to follow what was going on around us.

After four years in Taiwan I felt I had accomplished much and learnt many things including teaching English, editing ESL books, running a clothing business and selling on the night market. I felt pretty satisfied with what my life in Taiwan had given me.

I decided to return to Australia to gain a new experience, which was to study at university. However, before I returned to become a student, I decided that since I was now competent enough in Mandarin, I would first travel in mainland China. I initially planned to backpack around China for three months, but those three months extended into a year.

These travels in China provided great practice for my Mandarin. Not only did my Mandarin become better and better, I was able to recognise the different accents and subtle vocabulary differences from province to province. I managed to travel around most of China, and when I was in some of the very remote areas there were times when I did not speak English for several weeks.

Until this journey in China, I had not realised that I had learnt to read and write the traditional Chinese characters that are used in Taiwan. In mainland China simplified Chinese characters are used. The difference is that traditional Chinese characters use many more strokes than the simplified Chinese characters. In the mid-20th century, 2,200 Chinese characters were simplified, making the characters easier to read and write.

In mainland China I was also introduced to the Pinyin system, which is now used on street signs, menus, in train stations and on all manner of everyday signage.

When I returned to Australia, this knowledge of Mandarin and my experience living in Taiwan and mainland China made me somewhat special, although at that time I had no clear idea about how I would use my skills.

What is Face

*T*he concept of 'face' is a significant and deeply-held cultural value in Chinese culture. 'Face' can be thought of as a metaphor for a person's reputation. The Chinese concept of 'face' is different to the Western notion of 'self-esteem'. Self-esteem is centred around 'how I feel about myself', whereas 'face' is more to do with 'what other people think about me'. 'Face' involves social interaction and the exchange of information.

In Chinese society it is important to be respected by the group to which you belong, as the focus is on an individual's position within his/her own social group. 'Face' is gained, lost, or given in the presence of others. A Chinese person's reputation rests on how much 'face' he or she gains. The amount of 'face' a person has is a significant factor in defining a Chinese person's place in their social network.

The importance of 'face' is very relevant in Chinese business. In Book Two *Deceive the Dragon: Negotiating to retain power* we discussed personal relationships known as *guanxi*. Guanxi is about developing and maintaining relationships. In the development and maintenance of these vital relationships it is important to help each other save 'face'. Giving 'face' is a tool that is frequently used in creating new social connections. To keep 'face', Chinese business people will usually be non-confrontational, preferring indirect communication.

Strategies for Attack

*I*n Book Three *Lure the Tiger: Negotiating in confronting circumstances* you will learn about Strategies 13 - 18. These are known as the **Strategies for Attack**. The **Strategies for Attack** range from surveillance and concealment of the strategist's intentions, to making a direct move towards their counterpart in order to provoke a reaction. These strategies are resources to use when one is in a superior position, where planning and applying pressure become key elements. The objective in the negotiation is to weaken the counterpart before making a move to negotiate.

It is important to understand that Strategies 13 - 18 are a means of convincing your counterpart to provide you with the information that you are seeking. This can be achieved through a range of situations as you will read throughout Book Three – *Lure the Tiger: Negotiating in confronting circumstances.* These strategies reflect a manipulative technique, because the strategies aim to confuse and unsettle your counterpart.

Strategies
for Attack

Beat the grass to startle the snake *means "to create a situation that will provoke a revealing response"*

When you cannot detect the opponent's plans launch a direct, but brief, attack and observe your opponent's reactions. His behaviour will reveal his strategy.

*I*n the county of Jian-zhou a prominent man had lost a precious stone. He suspected that this stone had been stolen by one of the residents in the county, and he needed help to find the suspect. The best person to help him investigate the disappearance of his much loved treasure was Chen, who was the local magistrate in the county.

Although Chen questioned several suspects, none of them confessed, and he '*could not detect*' the thief, so he '*launched a direct, but brief, attack and he observed the suspects' reactions*'. Chen applied Strategy Thirteen – **Beat the grass to startle the snake** in the hope that the guilty man's behaviour would reveal the truth.

Chen applied Strategy Thirteen by bringing the county temple bell into the courthouse. The suspects were lined up and Chen told them the temple bell had spiritual powers, and that this bell would be able to reveal the person who stole the precious stone. He instructed them to touch the bell, and told them that if the person who touched the bell was innocent the bell would remain silent. However if the person who stole the precious stone was guilty, the bell would ring when touched. Curtains were placed around the bell and Chen then had his assistant paint the bell with ink.

Each suspect was told to reach their hands through the curtains covering the temple bell and place their hands gently on the bell for the count of ten. After touching the bell the magistrate examined their hands. Suspects who had touched the bell as instructed had ink stains on their hands, but one suspect's hands were not stained with ink. It was obvious to Chen who was guilty of stealing the precious stone, because it was this person who was too afraid to touch the temple bell for fear of it ringing. Therefore, the guilty person's hands were not stained with ink. The person with no ink on their hands had only one option, and that was to confess to the crime.

When Strategy Thirteen is used, the strategist creates a situation to provoke a response from their suspect, opponent, counterpart or anyone else from whom they want to elicit a reaction that will reveal their actions. This is done by placing them in a situation where they will be caught off guard.

Negotiating with Chinese People

EXAMPLE ONE
Strategy Thirteen in action (against you)

Chinese business people will apply Strategy Thirteen to see if you are afraid of opportunities that have the possibility of developing into something much larger than originally anticipated. For many Western business people, business deals and the overall size of China are larger than they could ever imagine. This can be quite daunting. When you visit China and are introduced to Chinese business people who show interest in your product, one of the ways Chinese business people apply Strategy Thirteen is to ask you if they can purchase a ridiculously large amount of your product. The amount they request is usually impossible for you to deliver in the time frame they request.

The application of Strategy Thirteen is to '*observe your reactions*'. The Western approach is to communicate in a direct style and to be up-front about your business's capacity by politely stating it is not possible to produce this amount in the time frame. When you react in this Western way your '*behaviour will reveal*' your non-understanding of Chinese culture, which may result in your Chinese contact becoming reluctant to do business with you.

Western people often do not understand that the application of Strategy Thirteen has nothing to do with reality. Instead, it is applied to '*observe your reactions*'. The Chinese person is testing you to see if you are afraid of large-scale business deals. Your reaction to unfamiliar situations may indicate that you would seek to avoid what might be unexpected opportunities. The opportunistic nature of Chinese business culture is seen in Strategy Twelve – **Seize the opportunity to lead a sheep away,** where the strategist takes advantage of any opportunity that presents itself. This is discussed in Book Two – *Deceive the Dragon: Negotiating to retain power* most Chinese business people are constantly looking for opportunities.

An excellent way to gain an introduction to Chinese business people is to travel to China on a business trade mission. This style of introduction means you will be travelling with several other businesses. Strategy Thirteen may be applied to each business in the group. The business that does not respond in a direct manner, and therefore does not close off opportunities, will most likely be the business the Chinese contact will want to work with. This is because people who come from an opportunistic culture will want to deal with a Western business person who is not afraid of opportunities, and who is willing to perceive the bigger picture. In order to capture every opportunity, Chinese business people are constantly saying 'yes' to everything – even if the request appears to be impossible – because by saying 'no' they may be closing the door to a potential opportunity.

Example One
Guarding yourself against Strategy Thirteen

To guard yourself against Strategy Thirteen simply know that this strategy is likely to be in action if you have been asked to do something that you feel is out of your normal scope of business. Think about how you could react, and therefore plan what you will say if Strategy Thirteen is applied on you, as it is not a good idea to say a direct 'no'. Your answer can be indirect, however it can still mean 'no'. If someone asks you for an outrageously large order that you cannot possibly fulfil, do not be afraid. Do not say an outright 'no', and do not show a nervous attitude. Indicate your interest in the request. Say how exciting filling this huge order will be and how much you are looking forward to doing business with your Chinese counterpart.

Example Two
Strategy Thirteen in action (against you)

Strategy Thirteen is often used when a Chinese delegation visits an educational institution. This educational institution might be a university that is very well prepared for the arrival of the delegation. Chinese delegations are usually quite large with up to twenty delegates. Large delegations can be a challenge for Western organisations to manage.

The delegates are shown around the campus and they discuss how impressed they are with what they see and how they would like to work together. The university hosting the delegation hopes to recruit more Chinese students as this will be good for the organisation's revenue base.

It is common practice that on the evening of the delegates' visit to the campus, the staff who work in the university's international recruitment department will host a dinner for the delegates. The situation may be that the university is in the middle of the city and the restaurant is a short walk from the campus, so the hosts decide to escort the Chinese delegates to the restaurant. This is also a great way for the Chinese delegates to enjoy the city in the evening. It is likely that prior to applying Strategy Thirteen, Strategy Two - **Besiege Wei to rescue Zhao** from Book One - *Tame the Tiger: Negotiating from a position of power* will be put into action. Strategy Two is about splitting the host group up so that individual hosts are walking alone with several Chinese delegates. The Chinese delegates will then apply Strategy Thirteen on an individual by asking if the university will accept 500 new Chinese students within the next two months, which would be impossible to accommodate.

The person on whom Strategy Thirteen is being enacted becomes very nervous as they know the university does not have the resources to handle this many new international students in such a short time frame. They also do not want to offend the Chinese delegates. They have been isolated through the application of Strategy Two and therefore there is no one to help them. The person wants to tell the truth and yet not offend or disappoint the Chinese delegates, who are watching and '*observing their reaction*'.

Example Two
Guarding yourself against Strategy Thirteen

In this situation remain calm because the Chinese delegation will never be able to send 500 students within two months. It would be impossible to organise the right visas and finalise all the paperwork required by the Chinese government within this time frame for each student to be able to study internationally.

The best answer for this situation would be that the university is interested in talking more about this, as your university has many Chinese students who are very satisfied with their programs and future job prospects on completion of their studies. Continue by saying that you will talk more about this excellent idea. In this way the Chinese delegation's outrageous proposal only ever ends up being talk. It does not become regarded as a reality by either party.

By responding in a way that treats the startling request with equanimity and respect, it will convey to your Chinese counterpart that you can handle anything and you are able to remain calm even when difficult questions are put to you. Your behaviour will show your Chinese contacts that you are someone they will want to work with.

Key Points when Strategy Thirteen is used against you

- The application of Strategy Thirteen usually has nothing to do with reality; it is applied to observe your reactions.
- The Chinese person is testing you; they want to deal with a Western business person who is not afraid of unplanned and unknown opportunities.
- Do not feel the need to say 'no' immediately to a large request; instead indicate your interest, as by saying 'no' you may be closing the door to a good contact.

EXAMPLE THREE
Enacting Strategy Thirteen

One situation where you would use Strategy Thirteen is if you want to find out if your Chinese contact is serious about what you have offered them.

It might be that you have implemented some specialised technology into a Chinese textile factory, which has made production easier and more efficient. However, this implementation was ten years ago and the technology needs significant upgrading to stay in line with the latest improvements. When the technology was first implemented you were very well connected with the owner of the factory who is a well-educated Chinese person. He has been very pleased with the technology as it has greatly improved the productivity and profitability of the factory. Consequently, this factory owner was generous with his purchases from you of minor upgrades to keep the factory running smoothly.

Three years ago the factory was sold. There is a new factory owner with whom you do not have strong *guanxi*. Further, this owner has demonstrated no interest in spending the money required for the readily available minor upgrades, and consequently problems have developed.

These problems are now so serious that there are days when the whole factory is shut down, and overall production has reduced. You know that the current technology is ten years old and needs completely replacing. With the implementation of newly developed technology these problems could be eliminated, production significantly improved and the factory's problems solved. While the upfront investment would be large, the savings in the long term would be significant.

You want to know whether it is worth you communicating with the factory owner, as he may be going to let the factory run down and you would be wasting your time. You know that if you are able to implement the new technology it will give you a good reputation across similar factories in China, and you will also gain significant 'face'. The only way that you will get to upgrade the system is if the new owners are interested in the long-term future of the factory. The new owner may not be interested if he has acquired the factory for the short-term only.

So you need to know if you are wasting your time. To apply Strategy Thirteen, you write him a detailed proposal outlining your ideas and noting the savings for him. Then you '*observe his reactions*' as '*his behaviour will reveal his strategy*'.

If he replies indicating interest in the technology, you will know he is interested in a long-term future for the factory under his ownership. If he does not respond or indicate any interest, then you will know there is no point in wasting your time.

Negotiating in a Western Environment

EXAMPLE FOUR
Enacting Strategy Thirteen

Strategy Thirteen is a strategy commonly used by lawyers. As an example, for some cease-and-desist letters the main objective is intimidation. This document represents an opportunity to '*attack and observe*' in order to elicit a response. When Strategy Thirteen is applied in this way the goal is for the person on whom the strategy is applied to back down. If a company or individual can scare you away by sending a lawyer's letter, they have successfully enacted Strategy Thirteen. These letters tend to identify very few facts about how you allegedly committed an illegal activity, but contain an alarming list of legal claims describing what they might have against you. The purpose of this move is to make you feel threatened, with the goal that you will react in the exact way the lawyers are predicting, which is to retreat.

Key Points when using Strategy Thirteen

- Decide what the information is that you wish to know. Strategy Thirteen may enable you to provoke a revealing reaction.
- Strategy Thirteen can be used to test your counterpart by exposing their reactions to your challenges.
- Observe and use the reactions of your counterpart to inform your next move.

Borrow a corpse to raise the spirit *means "to give a person or object a new purpose or reinterpretation"*

Take an institution, a technology, or a method that has been forgotten or discarded, and appropriate it for your own purpose. Revive something from the past by giving it a new purpose or reinterpret and bring to life old ideas, customs, and traditions.

*M*aster Li, who was a high-level well-respected meditation master discussed with one of his best students that his plan was to travel to heaven in spirit. He then planned to return his spirit to earth in seven days. He instructed this trustworthy student to look after his body during these seven days when his spirit was in heaven.

On the sixth day that the student was looking after Master Li's body, he received an urgent message that his mother was very ill, and he had to return to his home to look after her. He was worried that Master Li would not return to earth, so he made the decision to cremate Master Li's body and dispose of it. However, on the seventh day the Master did return from heaven to earth and could not find his body. His soul was floating around without a body so he applied

Strategy Fourteen - **Borrow a corpse to raise the spirit.**
Eventually he found the body of a beggar who had died by
the side of the road. Master Li's soul entered the beggar's
body, and by doing so he *'revived something from the past
by giving it a new purpose'.* The beggar's corpse was given a
new life.

When Strategy Fourteen is applied, the strategist uses a
person or an object which has been previously discarded
and gives it a new purpose. If Strategy Fourteen has been
applied on you it will be a challenge to detect if you are
dealing with a 'corpse', which is a person or thing that has
been *'revived from the past'.*

Negotiating with Chinese People

EXAMPLE ONE
Strategy Fourteen in action (against you)

Strategy Fourteen is often applied when Westerners are
visiting China and the Chinese contact wants to impress
the Westerner. The idea is to impress and influence you to
the point where you will be slightly intimidated by your
Chinese contacts because you are led to consider that their
status is higher than yours, and then they hope you will be
influenced to deal with their Chinese company. In preparing
yourself to go to China for a negotiation you may not see
what else is happening and find yourself seduced through
the application of Strategy Fourteen.

A situation in which Strategy Fourteen is applied on you
may be where you visit China to sell your wine to a contact

you met on a visit they made to your country. Your impression is that they are a small distributor. Their small size worries you a little. Your concern is that they may not have the necessary resources to market your wine. When you visit their offices you are surprised by the high quality displayed, as you did not expect this. What you did not realise is that your Chinese contacts have merely renovated the old offices they were in to impress you. They have '*revived something from the past by giving it a new purpose*'. It is likely that the perception you now have is that they are a large business in China with lots of resources for a business partnership. In reality, this is not the case. By giving themselves 'face' in front of you they are giving themselves higher status than they actually have.

There is also an underlying story, because they have developed very good *guanxi* with an expert builder and were able to get this renovation at a very good price. When they are applying Strategy Fourteen the idea is to convince you that they are the best people to work with. Not only do they want to convince you that they are the most prestigious people to work with, they want to influence you to give them a good price. You think that it is well worth giving them a good price because you are now convinced they are a bigger business than you previously thought. They have applied Strategy Fourteen successfully, because by '*reviving something from the past*' they have influenced you to work with them and give them a good price, as you are under the impression they are a high-status company with many resources.

EXAMPLE ONE
Guarding yourself against Strategy Fourteen

When visiting a Chinese contact, and in this case preparing to sell wine, do not be influenced by the appearance of their office environment. Do your background research on the company with whom you are planning to negotiate. If they have applied Strategy Fourteen they may not be what they appear to be. Once you see the situation more clearly, you may discover that Strategy Fourteen has been enacted on you. In this situation do not be overwhelmed by the new level of status that is being displayed. Understand that this scenario has been carefully thought through to impress you, so that you will think your Chinese contacts are the best business to deal with.

EXAMPLE TWO
Strategy Fourteen in action (against you)

When Strategy Fourteen is applied the objective the strategist is to ensure that you are actually dealing with someone or something that *'has been forgotten or discarded'*. The strategist uses this for their *'own purpose'*. A scenario may be that you are in a company that has expertise in building, managing and training in the area of aged care facilities. The Chinese company wants to buy the services of your company to build and manage a new aged care facility in Shanghai. You have visited China three times in the last year to negotiate with the Chinese company about the logistics of sending your staff to China, all of whom are experienced in the aged care sector. The staff will be required to go to China for one year.

The first time you visited China was with a group of businesses organised by your government. On that visit you were introduced to a large company in China that wants to build a modern aged care facility in Shanghai. The Chinese company has experience in aged care, but their experience in this sector is quite dated. They need the skills of a Western company like yours that has contemporary skills in the sector.

You were invited to return to China and it was on this second trip that you began negotiating costings and putting together a business structure. Prior to the trip you prepared many things so that you could discuss all the details, including how much preparation time your staff would require to relocate to China for the duration of the contract. After long discussions with the Chinese company you were happy with what was proposed and you decided on a suitable commencement date, as well as which staff you would send to China for the project. You allocate fifty staff to go to China in order for the project to be completed. The agreement you have made is that your staff will be accommodated in acceptable serviced apartments in Shanghai and will be funded to return for a visit to their home country once a year.

The plan is that you will return to China three months after your second visit to finalise preparation for the start date. Two weeks after you return from the second visit you are contacted by the Chinese company. They inform you they need you to return to China as soon as you can because the project needs to commence three months earlier than planned. You are told that this is due to the impact of new government regulations. They explain to you that they realise this is very inconvenient for you and your staff, and a new proposal will be presented to you that allows for this inconvenience.

So you return to China to meet with the company. You are then presented with what appears to be a new proposal. In this new proposal, your staff will be given two trips back to their home country each year, as opposed to the original offer of one trip. They will also be accommodated in more upmarket serviced apartments. The new proposal, which includes photographs of the new apartments, is printed on very good quality paper and bound into a book. The previous proposal lacked photographs and was on cheap paper just stapled together.

You accept the new conditions and agree to the earlier project start date. The next day you take a taxi to the 'new' serviced apartments and realise that they are actually the same style of apartments in the previous proposal, however of slightly lower quality.

Although the proposal contains a second flight home, it is the accommodation that is most important to the staff. While the second proposal seemed as though it had better conditions, it is actually the same proposal. It has just been written on better paper and with attractive photographs of the apartments. Worse, the apartments featured in the brochure are of a lower quality than the ones you originally agreed on, which you saw in person rather than simply as photographs. You also find out that the Chinese company runs a travel business, which means they can book the second trip for your staff at very cheap prices. They have simply revised the old proposal and presented it as the new proposal.

EXAMPLE TWO
Guarding yourself against Strategy Fourteen

To guard yourself against this situation, it is important to check everything before you agree on a proposal. What you are signing may be the old idea made to look as if you are getting something new and completely different. You need to look beyond the glossy photographs and presentation folder so you can see whether or not it is substantially the same proposal that you were first offered.

Before signing anything it is always good practice to check that what they are saying has changed has, in fact, changed. In the case of the apartments, it was only the glossy photographs that made them look good. In reality, they were lower quality apartments in the same block as previously proposed. Most things in the new proposal were revived from the previous proposal. You were actually not getting anything special or new, but you now have the inconvenience of bringing the project forward by several months, and your staff accommodation is not going to be as good.

Key Points when Strategy Fourteen is used against you

- Strategy Fourteen is often used to impress you so that the price you are negotiating becomes irrelevant.
- Do not respond to what seems like new surroundings as the situation may just be the same as the previous surroundings.
- Check everything before agreeing to a new proposal, as it may be the original proposal which now looks like it is new.

EXAMPLE THREE
Enacting Strategy Fourteen

When receiving Chinese delegations, Western people often think they have to keep presenting a new itinerary to each Chinese delegation. The purpose of this is to impress them and to build a solid reputable relationship. Many Western people have difficulty understanding the size of China with its 1.3 billion people. Even if the same Western city receives Chinese delegates every week, it is highly unlikely that the visiting groups will know each other, and therefore will not be aware of groups that have previously visited your city. This means you do not have to present a new itinerary and spend time and money thinking of different places to visit and new activities for each individual group.

By presenting the same itinerary to each group you are giving the itinerary '*a new purpose*', as this will be seen differently by each group. The best way to organise this, when receiving several Chinese delegations, is to work on one interesting itinerary which will only require minor adjustments for each visiting delegation.

You can organise to see some impressive sights which are iconic to your city. Also, a list of restaurants that will suit any group and opportunities to go shopping, which Chinese people love to do. The minor adjustments will therefore only be in relation to the industry they are focusing on. If you have a group that are interested in exploring biotechnology you can organise visits to restaurants, sightseeing activities and shopping which will be in the set itinerary, and then just add into the itinerary the biotechnology meetings for that specific group. In this way, the itinerary is given '*a new purpose*' for each delegation.

By applying Strategy Fourteen you will save a lot of time and money. You will also become familiar with the parts of the itinerary that are set as it is used over and over again. Even in a rare situation where different groups of delegates do know each other, in Chinese culture people like to follow what other people have done. This is unlike Western people who want to have new and different experiences compared to their colleagues. Applying Strategy Fourteen when hosting visiting delegations is much more time and cost effective.

Negotiating in a Western Environment

EXAMPLE FOUR
Enacting Strategy Fourteen

Strategy Fourteen is about '*reviving something from the past by giving it a new purpose*', and this is evident in second-hand shops in Western countries. Many Western people shop in second-hand shops, which are often filled with treasures that others have cast off as trash. This gives the purchaser the opportunity to '*revive an item from the past*', and '*repurpose it*' for their own advantage. Digging through dusty, cluttered racks and shelves in a store of pre-owned goods that hold the fruits of the past is the ultimate opportunity to apply Strategy Fourteen. In Western culture this is summed up by the idiom, 'One person's trash is another person's treasure'.

Key Points when using Strategy Fourteen
- Do not spend time, money and effort thinking about how to create something 'new.'
- Look for ways of repurposing something for your own benefit.
- Often only minor adjustments are needed to make something useful across several situations/circumstances.

Lure the tiger down the mountain
means "to entice someone out of their comfort zone"

Never directly attack a well-entrenched opponent. Instead, lure him away from his stronghold and separate him from his source of strength.

Gaozu was the first Han Emperor of China. He planned to destroy the Xiongnu tribes who were annoying him because they continued to destroy his land in the northern territories. Before launching an attack on the Xiongnu tribes he needed to know how powerful they were so that he could prepare his troops to win the battle. Gaozu sent his men to secretly assess the resources and strength of the Xiongnu tribes. The Xiongnu tribes had been forewarned of Gaozu's plan to spy on them. To apply Strategy Fifteen – **Lure the tiger down the mountain,** when Gaozu's men spied on them, the Xiongnu tribes were in their own territory, and they hid their strongest men and healthiest horses, leaving only old men and withered livestock to be seen by Gaozu's spies.

Gaozu's spies returned with the news that the Xiongnu tribes looked very weak and would be easy to defeat. Gaozu was happy about this because defeating the Xiongnu tribes meant he would no longer have to worry about his land in the northern territories being destroyed. Gaozu organised an immediate attack on the Xiongnu tribes. His men were '*lured away*' from their familiar territory, which meant they were '*separated from their source of strength*', because they were going to battle in the Xiongnu tribe's territory. Being away from their familiar surroundings did not concern them because they thought they were up against weak opponents, and this would therefore be an easy battle for them to win.

When they arrived to commence the battle the Xiongnu tribes brought out their strongest men and fastest horses to fight Gaozu's army. This meant that Gaozu's army were now fighting a strong, experienced army in unfamiliar territory. Goazu's men had been '*lured away from their stronghold and separated from their source of strength*'. In this battle Gaozu's army were easily defeated and barely managed to escape the battle. The Xiongnu tribes continued to invade and destroy Gaozu's northern territories.

When Strategy Fifteen is applied, the objective of the strategist is to lure the opponent out of their comfort zone and into the strategist's territory. When the opponent is out of their comfort zone, they do not have access to their usual resources and hence the strategist has the advantage in the negotiation.

Negotiating with Chinese People

EXAMPLE ONE
Strategy Fifteen in action (against you)

Strategy Fifteen is used on you by creating a situation where you are '*separated from your source of strength*'. This strategy is applied in such a way that you do not notice you are being taken away from your location, and therefore your comfort zone. Many Westerners visit China regularly as they find this is a necessary part of building the relationship with their Chinese contacts. The seasoned travellers become quite confident as they begin to feel familiar with the city they regularly visit. Part of this familiarity comes from staying at the same hotel each time they visit China, which allows them to get to know a small area of a large city. They probably have a favourite restaurant they frequently eat at, and there may be a shopping mall nearby where Westerners can buy most things. Being familiar with parts of the city, the hotel, restaurants, and shopping areas all add up to a familiar experience for a Westerner, and therefore confidence is gained in a country that is very different to Western countries.

It is likely Strategy Fifteen will be applied on you in a scenario where you frequently visit a city such as Shanghai and have begun to feel comfortable in this location. The time then comes when you need to have an important meeting about pricing. As your contacts know you feel comfortable in Shanghai because you have always met with them there, to apply Strategy Fifteen they will try to *'lure you away from your stronghold and separate you from your source of strength'*. They may do this by inviting you to Beijing.

When inviting you to Beijing they do not talk about the meeting, they only talk about the wonderful hotel and the city sites. They offer to pay for a hotel that has a great view of the city and want to take you to see The Great Wall of China and other world-famous sights. You can be overwhelmed with all the new information you need to take in about your surroundings and forget that you are there to negotiate a deal. They are applying Strategy Fifteen by taking you out of your comfort zone, and into an unfamiliar location. The reality is that you will be in a city you are not familiar with, which will place you at a disadvantage when you have to discuss prices. Visiting places we are not familiar with requires us to invest a lot of effort into getting comfortable with the new location. When Strategy Fifteen is applied, and you are in an unfamiliar environment, the stress level this unfamiliarity causes, may mean you are more likely to give your contact a price that is to their advantage.

In this situation Strategy Fifteen is applied to lure you into unfamiliar territory, and the strategist is on their own familiar territory which inevitably places you at a disadvantage and them at an advantage. This means you are likely to accept a price for your product that is lower than you had anticipated.

EXAMPLE ONE
Guarding yourself against Strategy Fifteen

To guard yourself against Strategy Fifteen it is important to remember when you are offered sightseeing and luxury accommodation in an unfamiliar location, while this may look attractive it is in fact to *'lure you away from your stronghold,'* and therefore out of your comfort zone. In this situation you are the tiger and you are being lured down the mountain. When tigers move from the mountains onto the plains they are exposed and vulnerable. If you have rarely been to the city that you are being invited to, you need to suggest that it is more convenient for you to negotiate in the city you are familiar with. In this situation it would be Shanghai, as you have previously met with your contacts there.

To avoid being lured to a strange location, you may want to say that you have other meetings in the city you normally visit, and therefore you would prefer to have the meeting there. Explain to your contacts that you would be delighted to go to Beijing to see them next time you visit China. The next time you visit your contact, and you take up their offer to go to Beijing, be certain you are not there to negotiate something critical, like price, because such a negotiation will put you under a degree of tension. When you have to negotiate it is always better to avoid being in a new environment. The best scenario is to negotiate in the location where you feel most comfortable.

EXAMPLE TWO
Strategy Fifteen in action (against you)

A scenario may be that you are a water purification company and you have been communicating with a Chinese company about them purchasing your technology. You are aware that due to the environmental issues in China, your product will be sought after by a Chinese company. You were introduced to this company when they visited your city on a government inbound mission. The Chinese group that visited consisted of five people, and only one member of the group spoke English. When they visited on the government trade mission it was their first visit to your country.

Since then they have visited you twice and are very interested in your technology. The third visit is to discuss price and what is being included in that price, such as training on how to use the technology. You feel quite comfortable with the format because this will be conducted on your premises in a location you are familiar with. You will be able to provide demonstrations and will not be constrained by having to board a plane and leave at a specific time. The week before they arrive they contact you and suggest meeting at a resort in Singapore as they would also like to take some leisure time and socialise with you. They offer to pay for your airfares and accommodation at the resort. There is no problem about bringing the water purification prototypes, as they will pay for the transportation of these items. This seems like a wonderful offer, so you accept it. When you arrive at the resort in Singapore you realise that they own the resort and visit there regularly, which places them in familiar territory. They are also in a place where they speak the language, because many Singaporeans speak Mandarin Chinese Strategy Fifteen has been applied on you because you have been *'lured away from your stronghold'*, and therefore away from your familiar territory. This places you at a disadvantage for the negotiation. You have been taken out of your familiar territory and you also have to leave at a specific time. This Chinese group have not planned when they will leave the resort. In this situation, time is not on your side, therefore it is highly likely that you will give them a deal which is at a lower price than you originally planned.

Example Two
Guarding yourself against Strategy Fifteen

To guard yourself against Strategy Fifteen when your Chinese contacts invite you to another place to negotiate a deal, it is important that you research the place that you are being invited to prior to accepting the invitation. Things may seem very attractive and generous. However, you need to keep in mind that this is a business deal and there is a strategy in action. Research any connections that your Chinese contact may have in the place they have invited you to. In the above example, if you discover that they own the resort and you are going to a place that speaks their language you will probably be at a disadvantage. If your contact suggests you go to a different place to negotiate than the place where you originally planned to meet, you may want to push back and make your own suggestion about where the meeting should take place. Not only will this give you control, it will also put you in a position where both parties are in an unfamiliar environment. This then means you will be on equal terms and you will not be subordinate to them.

The most important thing is to research as much information as you can about the suggested location, and use this information to place yourself in a strong position. Do not just accept what is suggested to you by the Chinese company.

Key Points when Strategy Fifteen is used against you

- When conducting business with Chinese people, do not be lured by an invitation to appealing new cities or famous destinations unfamiliar to you.
- Try to avoid negotiating in a place that is not familiar to you, and remember the more familiar you are the more confident you will be.
- If you have to travel to a place that is unfamiliar, conduct research regarding the connections your Chinese contacts have to the suggested location.

EXAMPLE THREE
Enacting Strategy Fifteen

When applying Strategy Fifteen, the crucial component is to think of ways in which you can take your Chinese contact out of their comfort zone. One scenario may be where you have met a prospective Chinese buyer who wants to import your products into China. The products they want to import may come from any industry sector, but it will be easier to apply Strategy Fifteen on a business with a product that is sought after in China. This is because if your products are in high demand, the Chinese buyer will not need to be convinced about the benefits of your products, and they are likely to make the effort to leave China and negotiate in your country.

To apply Strategy Fifteen when preparing to discuss a deal and negotiate a price, you can invite your contact to your country where you will show them some world-famous tourist attractions. Chinese people will gain 'face' by visiting these famous sights, as they can tell their friends and family about their trip. For a Chinese person to gain 'face' they need to be respected in front of other people. By visiting a country that many Chinese people wish to visit, the person who goes to these locations will gain 'face' from their friends and family. 'Face' is a fundamental component of Chinese culture, and so to offer ways of gaining 'face' means you are likely to easily lure contacts away from their familiar location. In this way you have *lured them away from their stronghold and separated them from their source of strength*, which is their familiar location in China.

By enticing your Chinese contacts to negotiate on your territory you will place them at a disadvantage, as they will be in an unfamiliar location. They will be constrained by time, as they have to board a plane to travel home, while you will be able to stay in your own country. By manoeuvring them into an unfamiliar environment, they are likely to agree to a price that is more profitable and acceptable for you.

Negotiating in a Western Environment

EXAMPLE FOUR
Enacting Strategy Fifteen

In Western business, mediation is a dynamic, structured, interactive process where a neutral third party assists disputing parties in resolving conflict through the use of specialised communication and negotiation techniques. You can understand Strategy Fifteen through the use of mediation, as mediation can represent the means by which you *'lure the parties involved away from their stronghold.'* When mediation takes place on neutral ground, each party is taken away from their familiar environment and *'separated from their source of strength.'* Through the use of mediation you have removed each party from their comfort zone, which is away from their office environment and into another environment with which they are not familiar. By doing so, you allow both parties to achieve a sense of power. Therefore, you will be far more likely to control the situation and allow for fair and sensible negotiations to take place.

Key Points when using Strategy Fifteen

- Research the boundaries of your counterpart's comfort zone.
- Convince your counterpart to negotiate in a place unfamiliar to them by offering something attractive which they will find difficult to refuse.
- Influence your Chinese counterpart to go to your location by offering things that will give them 'face'.

To catch something, first let it go *means "to position someone in your debt while managing to keep their dignity"*

Cornered prey will often mount a final desperate attack. To prevent this, you let the enemy believe he still has a chance for freedom. His will to fight is thus dampened by his desire to escape. When in the end freedom is proven to be a falsehood, the enemy's morale will be defeated and he will surrender without a fight.

---

*D*uring the time of the Three Kingdoms, Zhu Ge Liang was the Prime Minister of Shu. He was highly regarded and perceived to be a great asset, because he was considered to be the master strategist of war. As he was such a great strategist, Zhu Ge Liang often had his time consumed in battles with different kings who were from many territories, and he always won the battle.

Menguo, who was the King of the Southern Tribe, had wanted to stand up to Zhu Ge Liang and hopefully defeat him, so he decided it was a good idea to join forces with the other leaders. His plan was that this joining of forces would provide a strong army that would be able to resist Zhu Ge Liang's rule. They joined their armies and marched towards Shu to commence a battle. However, their army was no match for Zhu Ge Liang's people because he had many highly-skilled strategic fighters.

On the first day of this battle Zhu Ge Liang used Strategy Sixteen - **To catch something first let it go** to capture Menguo and his army and keep them prisoners. It was surprising to Menguo because his army was treated with friendly hospitality while they were in captivity. Zhu Ge Liang offered them plenty of food and wine and a comfortable place to rest. Mengou still wanted to fight Zhu Ge Liang and informed Zhu Ge Liang that he would attack again. Despite Zhu Ge Liang being given this information, he released Mengou and his troops.

Mengou was true to his word and attacked Zhu Ge Liang again. Just as had happened previously, Mengou was captured. He was again treated with friendly hospitality by Zhu Ge Liang. Once again, Menguo said that as soon as he was released he would attack again, and this time he was determined to be successful. Zhu Ge Liang understood Mengou was a man of great pride, and he knew that for his own leadership there would be a better outcome if Mengou came to trust him, rather than feeling humiliated through being defeated outright in battle.

Mengou and his troops were released, and the same situation followed many times because he *'believed he still had the chance for freedom'*. After the seventh time Mengou finally realised how fortunate he was to be given so many opportunities and not to be defeated outright. He finally accepted that Zhu Ge Liang was the ruler and he promised never to resist his ruling again. In the end for Mengou *'freedom was a proven falsehood'* and he therefore *'surrendered without a fight'*.

When Strategy Sixteen is applied, the strategist will manoeuvre you into a position where you are in debt to them. However, this positioning is very calculated and you are left feeling no animosity towards them, because you will still have your dignity and will therefore continue to respect them.

Negotiating with Chinese People

EXAMPLE ONE
Strategy Sixteen in action (against you)

To apply Strategy Sixteen, your Chinese counterpart will have an objective: to win you over without losing your respect. They will '*dampen your desire*' to argue against them about price or anything else you are negotiating. Generally, Strategy Sixteen will be applied when you have made a mistake, which is often one of a cultural nature as this is likely to happen when you are in their country.

When invited to a dinner in China, Westerners often feel uneasy because they are not likely to be aware of the correct protocols when dining. China practices vastly different cultural rules from Western countries. These rules are based around hierarchy and are not to be ignored. A typical scenario may be where you are invited to a beautiful restaurant where you will meet your Chinese contacts, and it is a very important dinner because the head of the company will attend. This means you need to create a positive impression if you want to achieve a good selling price for your product. The following morning you will be meeting them at their office to discuss the deal further.

There are three people from your company attending the dinner, and no one is accustomed to the traffic in China. As a result, the time allocated to travel to the restaurant is misjudged. This lack of traffic knowledge makes you ten minutes late to meet your Chinese counterparts. You apologise profusely and your Chinese contacts say nothing and just smile. However, because they have said nothing you do not know where you stand, which makes you feel in debt to them. This situation places your team in an awkward position. The head person from your group then sits at the head of the table, which is where they would sit in a Western setting, not realising it is completely different in China. This is because in China the lowest person sits at the head of the table. The person of the highest ranking should sit at the middle of the table. This becomes the second mistake, and the person responsible apologies.

When everyone is seated and the dinner is in full swing, the Chinese group walks around the table clinking glasses with each person. Your team overlooks that when this happens, in order to give 'face', you must place your glass lower than the other person when they are offering to say cheers to you. Not placing the rim of your glass lower than the person from the Chinese group displays your ignorance of the cultural rules. The Chinese group continues to keep smiling and shows no emotion about what has happened. Over the course of the dinner you and your team realise that you have made several several cultural mistakes.

Preparing for the next day's meeting, you believe that it is a new day and you will not let yourself feel in debt to them. You believe you still have a chance to make a good impression. You enter their office the following morning, and after all of the mistakes you made at the dinner, they present you with a gift each and a gift for your company, and you have no gifts for them or their company. Now you really feel your '*morale is defeated*' and you are again put in the position of being in debt to them. You sit and discuss price and you give them the price they want by '*surrendering without a fight*'. You feel so indebted to them that you not only give them a good price but also some extras to further sweeten the deal.

EXAMPLE ONE
Guarding yourself against Strategy Sixteen

If you are late arriving to the restaurant due to poor judgement of traffic and time, do not apologise to your Chinese counterparts. Most Chinese people will understand that China is much busier than many Western countries and that traffic is difficult to avoid. However, it is better if you can avoid being late in the first place, so leave early enough to avoid a late arrival. Prior to going to China, research what the cultural rules are because they will be vastly different. Spend time with a consultant who understands this and can prepare you for your trip.

'Face' is a very important component of Chinese culture and you need to know the boundaries around when you are giving 'face' and possibly causing a 'loss of face'. If you do happen to make cultural mistakes, such as sitting in the wrong place at the table or not lowering the rim of your glass when a toast is being made do not apologise, just continue on as if nothing has happened. If you show emotion about these mistakes you will place yourself in debt to your Chinese counterparts. When you are in debt, your Chinese counterparts have successfully applied Strategy Sixteen. If you enter the meeting and they have a gift and you do not, there is nothing you can do about the situation, just gratefully accept the gift and sit down for the meeting. Do not let this situation make you feel as though you have to give them a price that you are not happy with. Often when Strategy Sixteen is applied, Western people feel in debt to their Chinese counterparts. To guard against Strategy Sixteen, do not let their actions make you feel that you owe them something.

Example Two
Strategy Sixteen in action (against you)

A scenario may involve a Chinese group visiting your country. The city you live in has a 'sister city' relationship with a city in China. These sister city relationships are important and should be treated very seriously. Your city's officials invited you to be part of the team welcoming and entertaining these Chinese guests. You have been chosen as one of the twenty businesses that will be involved with providing entertainment over the three days the Chinese delegates are visiting your city. As is often the case with these things, because the organisers get very busy you do not have a lot of preparation time. Also, as you are one of twenty businesses, it is impossible for much of the focus to be on you alone.

You are aware that the Chinese visitors are representing government and private sector areas of China. They are interested in investment opportunities, and also want to find out more about importing products to China. This appears to be a perfect opportunity because you own a winery, and you are thinking in the first instance that you can export your wine to China, and then in the future you would like to possibly sell your winery. You are given the opportunity to present, but you have not really prepared for any of the questions that they may ask, such as "*Can we own property in your country?*" "*What are the visa regulations?*" or "*If I do not speak much English, and I want to purchase your winery, how can I employ people who only speak English*?"

When you feel as though you lack knowledge about these important questions '*your desire is dampened*' to negotiate the price you want. Your '*morale is defeated*', and instead of focusing on the fact that you have an excellent business to sell you are seduced by their passive behaviours when they do not question your lack of knowledge. To simply get their trust you offer your winery for a lower price than it is worth, and also give them several bottles of wine. You do this because you feel in debt to them as they have travelled from China and you were not able to answer their questions. Strategy Sixteen was successfully applied because they did not inform you that it did not matter that you could not answer their questions. They just kept asking politely and repeating the questions, which '*dampened your desire*' to offer them the price you really want. This situation leaves you feeling in debt to them '*and you surrender without a fight*' in order to keep your dignity.

EXAMPLE TWO
Guarding yourself against Strategy Sixteen

Remember it is important to prepare for questions that your Chinese contacts might ask, because when applying Strategy Sixteen they are aware you probably cannot answer the questions put to you. The more you are asked questions that are outside your scope of knowledge, and demonstrate a slight anxiety because you do not know the answers to these questions, the more you give your Chinese contacts the opportunity to apply Strategy Sixteen. Be confident and tell them that you will find the answers to their questions. Even if it takes a few days you will get back to them with an appropriate answer. This will give you confidence, and also a chance to apply Strategy Twelve – **Seize the opportunity to lead a sheep away,** from Book Two – *Deceive the Dragon: Negotiating to retain power*. By offering to get the answers to their questions builds your *guanxi*, which means you are continuing to explore opportunities. Then you have not only guarded yourself against Strategy Sixteen, you have also applied Strategy Twelve. By stating you will get back to them with an answer you gain the upper hand and put yourself in a position to ask for the price you want.

> **Key Points when Strategy Sixteen is used against you**
> - Be confident when you are asked a question you do not have the answer to. Research the answer and get back to your Chinese counterpart.
> - Research the cultural boundaries or seek professional advice before going to China to conduct business.
> - If you make a cultural mistake do not apologise, just continue to move forward.

EXAMPLE THREE
Enacting Strategy Sixteen

The main purpose of Strategy Sixteen is to gain the trust of the person or people whom you are applying this strategy on. For Strategy Sixteen to work successfully, when applied, your Chinese counterparts will feel in debt to you. When they are in this position you will be able to do business with them with ease and confidence.

There are many exhibitions in China. In fact, whatever product you are planning to export to China, you can be almost certain there will be an exhibition for your product to be displayed to a large audience. In a situation where you are in the business of gemstones such as opals, and you want to set up a stand at an exhibition, for you to apply Strategy Sixteen you need to plan to give away a reasonably valuable gift. For this gift you will want something in return. The

Chinese visitors are not obligated to give you anything, but if Strategy Sixteen works they will feel in debt to you and will want to give you what you have requested.

You can organise some opal gifts such as lapel pins with a small opal stone that they can pin to their clothes, and when they accept the lapel pins you can explain you would like them to attend your presentation. The objective of the presentation is to showcase your opals, and ultimately to sell your product. All of the attendees sit in your presentation with their opals pinned to their clothing. This then gives you the opportunity to take a photo and request their contact details so that you can send copies of the photo to them, which means you then have their contact details. If Strategy Sixteen is applied with careful consideration, they will feel in debt to you and they will want to attend your presentation. They will *surrender without a fight*. You will have created two situations. The first is that they come to see your presentation, and the second is you get their contact details.

Negotiating in a Western Environment

Example Four
Enacting Strategy Sixteen

Strategy Sixteen can be enacted in a Western business environment when you need to penalise an employee for poor work performance. A scenario may be that you give an employee a large task to complete and they do not follow through with completing this task. To apply Strategy Sixteen do not reprimand them in the moment when you are feeling angry or disappointed, because if you take this approach it is likely they may feel threatened, get defensive and lose respect for you. However, you still want the employee to know that you are disappointed in them and their level of work performance. So you take them out for a coffee to discuss the problem. As a result of applying Strategy Sixteen you have '*dampened their desire*' to get defensive and it is likely they will now be far more willing to accept responsibility and '*surrender without a fight*'. You are rewarding the employee in a small way by treating them to coffee and giving some of your precious time. It is probable that they will now feel more loyalty to you, and as a result it will be more likely that they will follow through with the tasks you give them in the future.

Key Points when using Strategy Sixteen

- Create a situation where the person you are marketing to feels as though they owe you something.
- When at an exhibition, give away something of value and then you can take your potential customer to the next phase of your product introduction.
- When wanting to change an employee's behaviour reward them in a small way before telling them what you are not happy with.

Strategy Seventeen

Toss out a brick to attract jade *means "trade something of minor value for something of higher value"*

Prepare a trap then lure your enemy into the trap by using bait. In war, the bait is the illusion of an opportunity for gain. In life, the bait is the illusion of wealth, power, and sex.

*D*uring the Hang Dynasty General Li Mu was sent north in order to deal with the Xiongnu nomads who were causing many problems. The north was covered in grassland, and every time the general attempted to battle the Xiongnu they would quickly run away into the thick grassland. General Li Mu wanted to get them out of hiding and into an actual battle. His plan was to win the battle so he would never have to deal with them again. He would do this by applying Strategy Seventeen - T**oss out a brick to attract jade** and luring them out of the grasslands, because he wanted to *'lure his enemy into the trap by using bait'*.

General Li Mu ordered his entire army to go southward. To the Xiongnu nomads this manoeuvre looked like General Li Mu's troops were retreating. He applied Strategy Seventeen by devising a situation that showed the Xiongnu nomads *'the illusion of an opportunity for gain'*. He purposely positioned the baggage train travel quite a distance behind his troops. As the days passed the baggage train got further and further behind his army. The Xiongnu nomads began to notice that not only was the baggage train getting further and further away from General Li Mu's army, it was also getting less well guarded. While following it, the Xiongnu nomads carefully planned to steal its contents by attacking the baggage train when they felt it was clearly out of reach of General Li Mu's army.

As General Li Mu troops were ahead of the baggage train they had reached a fork in the road, which was surrounded by mountains and hills. At this fork in the road General Li Mu had his most skilled troops hide in different positions while the rest of his army continued to march ahead. Once the baggage train reached this fork in the road it slowed to a stop. The Xiongnu thought General Li Mu's army was now far away, and they decided it was time to loot the contents of the baggage train. Once they were in the process of stealing the contents, the general and his troops attacked the Xiongnu nomads from many directions, and they finally defeated them. General Li Mu was happy with the result because the Xiongnu nomads caused no more trouble to his people.

To apply Strategy Seventeen General Li Mu sacrificed the contents of his baggage train. As these contents were of little value to him he freely gave them up. However, the Xiongnu nomads were resource poor, and for them the baggage train contents were of high value. What General Li Mu planned to get in return for giving up the contents of his baggage train was close proximity to the Xiongnu nomads. When the Xiongnu nomads went to loot the baggage train they were attacked from all directions by General Li Mu's army. What seemed like such a large thing to the Xiongnu nomads was in fact a small price for General Li Mu to pay in order to be able to control future actions of the Xiongnu nomads.

When Strategy Seventeen is applied, the strategist gives away something which is of little value to them in order to get something of high value in return. Strategy Seventeen may look very similar to Strategy Sixteen – **To catch something, first let it go**. However, Strategy Seventeen and Strategy Sixteen are quite different. In Strategy Sixteen the strategist creates a situation where the person or group they are dealing with are in some way indebted to the strategist, which often puts them in a position where they feel they should give the strategist something in return.

Negotiating with Chinese People

EXAMPLE ONE
Strategy Seventeen in action (against you)

When Strategy Seventeen is applied on you, you are put in a situation where you feel you are gaining something of value. However, what you are gaining is not of a high value to the strategist. When conducting business with Chinese companies, foreign companies often use the joint venture structure. If all parties are able to benefit and communicate in a clear way, the joint venture structure works well. When the business model is a joint venture there is often a need for the Western company to have a physical presence in China, and sometimes they will also need to send staff to work in the China office. Most Western business people have heard that office space in large Chinese cities such as Guangzhou, Shanghai and Beijing is very expensive. A scenario may be that the Chinese company with whom you are doing the joint venture informs you that they can organise office space for you in the Shanghai Central Business District (CBD) and they will pay the rent. You have researched the price of office space in Shanghai and soon realise that it is very expensive Your joint venture partner's offer seems like a very good deal, as you are aware that you could not find office space in Shanghai CBD at a low price, and so to have the space provided free of charge seems wonderful. As they are paying the rent for the office the deal is that your company puts two staff in the China office and pays for all the expenses related to these members of staff. You quickly agree to the deal. Unfortunately, you are not familiar with the concept of *guanxi* and have not done your research regarding what this really means. The company that you are doing business with has strong *guanxi* in the location of this office space. They have *guanxi* with the owners of the office block so they are able to get the rent at a very cheap price.

They have '*lured you into the trap by using bait*'. The bait is what seems to be a very expensive office space that makes you feel like you are getting a great deal. You perceive that the cost of this office in Shanghai will outweigh what you spend to send two staff to Shanghai to be located in the China office. When Strategy Seventeen is applied, '*this is the illusion of an opportunity for gain*. However, this 'free office space' is only an illusion because what you are giving back to them, two of your staff, is really far greater than what they are giving you.

Example One
Guarding yourself against Strategy Seventeen

When Strategy Seventeen is applied you are presented with *'the illusion of an opportunity for gain'*. The most crucial thing to be aware of when Strategy Seventeen is applied is that if you are being be offered something that seems to be of value, the value may be an illusion. What you are being offered will often appear difficult for you to acquire which will add to the sense that it is worth having. In the case of being given free rent in the Shanghai CBD in exchange for placing staff in the office, before accepting the deal research how your contact is able to make this offer. Their level of *guanxi* is likely to be the reason they can offer you such a good deal. Research who they have *guanxi* with. When the deal looks too good to be true be careful, as Chinese people are good negotiators and are unlikely to pay for something that is usually very expensive, without expecting something valuable in return.

Guanxi plays an important role in China and in most deals there is a place that *guanxi* has an influence. Even when you have decided to embark on a joint venture and everything seems to be going smoothly it is important that you continue to negotiate, because when dealing with China negotiation never stops. Be calm and do not just jump into a deal without taking the time to satisfy yourself that it is advantageous. If you find out later that you have invested a lot more than your joint venture partner, then you are likely to resent your partner. When doing business with Chinese people you are expected to research and not just accept what they offer. Research and pushing back is normal negotiating behaviour, especially when dealing with Chinese business people.

EXAMPLE TWO
Strategy Seventeen in action (against you)

In Strategy Seventeen the strategist focuses on the concept that the value of the object or idea they are giving away is relative to each individual or company. When applying Strategy Seventeen what is of value to you is not of a high value to the strategist. The skill in applying Strategy Seventeen is firstly to identify what is important to the person who is receiving what the strategist offers. This information is thoroughly researched, so it is almost impossible for the receiver to refuse what is being offered. In fact, sometimes what you are offered looks 'too good to be true'. Think twice when you are offered such a great deal because it probably is 'too good to be true' and will merely be *the illusion for an opportunity for gain*.

A situation may be that your job is to organise the importing of shirts for a large department store in your country. The main role of your position as the import manager is to organise the purchasing of merchandise from China, and of course to achieve the best deal possible. Your company already imports merchandise from three companies in China, and you have done an excellent job at developing relationships and building trust with these Chinese companies. Over the years you have gained considerable respect in your company, as a result of the deals you have established with these Chinese companies.

So far, things have gone smoothly. Even though things are going well it is important to continually search out new suppliers as there is no guarantee that the three Chinese companies will continue to operate. You search for these new suppliers at exhibitions, where you can see examples of the merchandise. You meet a new supplier at a textiles exhibition in Guangzhou who has an impressive booth, which means you are able to view their products first hand. You have done your research and cross-checked the Chinese company with your in-China government offices. The advice is that this company is trustworthy and reliable, and very shrewd in their business dealings. You consider yourself pretty good at doing business in China as you have been doing this for a while. The thing that is missing in your knowledge is an understanding of how the 36 Strategies are used.

This Chinese company has high-quality shirts, which is a step-up from what you have been importing from the other three companies. Although their prices are higher they offer you a very good deal. The deal they offer is that if you purchase 1,000 shirts you will get 100 free. Even though their standard price is higher, what they offer you makes the price slightly lower than the other three companies. You enter into this deal and you assume that you will always be presented with this deal, which would mean never paying full price. However, the company did not confirm this structure. On the basis of developing trust and a solid relationship with the company you do not question how long this deal will last. The only thing the company have stated is 'we will look after you', and that statement is enough for you to accept the deal. You do not want to question this because you are afraid your questioning will damage the *guanxi* you have so diligently developed.

To apply Strategy Seventeen, the Chinese company gives you 100 free shirts when you purchase 1000 shirts. Over a six-month period you place three large orders to import these shirts and everything is going well. The shirts are cheaper and better quality, the stock arrives on time and there is customer satisfaction as your customers recognise the good quality. After six months, once the product is embedded into your store, the price goes back to normal, which is now much higher than you pay with the other Chinese suppliers. They have '*lured you into a trap by using bait*' by providing high-quality, low-priced stock. This now places your company in an awkward position. In order to continue to provide customer satisfaction you will probably have to keep buying from this Chinese supplier. Also, you will now have to reconsider your end price, because the profit margin on each shirt will be lower. The Chinese company have successfully applied Strategy Seventeen, because they have a customer who now has to pay them at their normal price. The risk in not dealing with the Chinese company is that you will lose customers from your store, because these customers are now used to the higher quality. In fact, in the six months you have been dealing with this company, you have purchased less from the other three Chinese companies. There is the possible risk that you have now damaged the solid *guanxi* you have with the other three Chinese companies.

In this situation Strategy Seventeen has been successfully applied. The result of the success of Strategy Seventeen is that Strategy Eight – **Openly repair the walkway, secretly march to Chencang,** which is explained in Book Two – *Deceive the Dragon: Negotiating to retain power* is now also being applied, as Strategy Eight is being used to help the company enter a new territory with their product.

Example Two
Guarding yourself against Strategy Seventeen

Often when Strategy Seventeen is applied the deal appears to be very attractive. You may even feel as though you have won a battle in the challenging Chinese market. This kind of feeling is evidence that Strategy Seventeen has been applied on you. Do not be disappointed if you discover before the transaction goes ahead that what you are actually giving back to the strategist is more than they are giving you, even though you thought otherwise. It is important that you are aware of the full extent of the unevenness in the transaction before you agree to any deals. Remember, when Strategy Seventeen is applied you are being '*lured into a trap by using bait*'. The bait generally involves something that is very attractive to your business development. In the case of the Chinese clothing supplier, a more effective management of the situation would have been to clarify if the 100 shirts deal was going to run out, and if so, when would this happen. This could have been achieved by asking the question, "*How long will you give us this deal*"?

Be aware, when such a straightforward question is presented Strategy Six – **Make a noise in the east and attack in the west** from Book One – *Tame the tiger: Negotiating from a position of power* is likely to be applied. Strategy Six is used to shift the focus of the conversation. A better plan would have been to continue to purchase from the three Chinese suppliers you have already established relationships with, as they have proven to be stable regarding price. Careful thought needs to be applied to work through the implications of Strategy Seventeen when it is successfully applied. In this case, the results included a more expensive end price of the garment, which means the end price in the department store needs to be higher in order to continue the acceptable profit margin. Additionally, you do not want to weaken your relationship with the existing Chinese suppliers.

Key Points when Strategy Seventeen is used against you
- If a deal looks 'too good to be true' it probably is, because Chinese business people are expert negotiators.
- If you feel that you have won a deal easily, examine the situation closely for potential risks.
- Do not be afraid to ask how long the deal you are offered will last.

EXAMPLE THREE
Enacting Strategy Seventeen

As the middle class grows in China and there is more surplus money, more Chinese people are travelling to Western countries. Often when they visit Western countries they experience a more attractive lifestyle that includes less crowded places and environments with cleaner air. Sometimes after visiting these places Chinese people plan to move from China to live permanently in these locations. It is common for them to use a specialised property agent who has experience in the Chinese market to assist them in buying a suitable house. This property agent is in an excellent position to apply Strategy Seventeen. Property agents are often connected with businesses that will add value to a property by including landscapers and professional gardeners. In China, most people live in high-rise apartments and often have little or no experience in establishing and maintaining a front and back yard of a house.

To apply Strategy Seventeen a property agent could use their connections with people who are specialised in creating attractive outside spaces. They could offer the Chinese buyer one-year free garden development and maintenance with the purchase of the property. To offer this deal it is likely the property agent would get a much better price from the Chinese buyer. Also, if they are well connected with gardening businesses, they may be able to get a good price for such a project. This offer would give the potential Chinese buyer '*the illusion of an opportunity for gain*' because they are likely to know very little about how much this service would cost, simply because it is rare to use such a service in China.

In this situation, to make the application of Strategy Seventeen even stronger, the property agent could offer the Chinese buyers an educational element where they can learn about how to look after their garden. This would be giving away something of minor value for something of major value, which is the sale of the property. Having an attractive garden and knowing how to look after it would give the Chinese buyers 'face' in front of their neighbours and their Chinese friends. In Western countries when Chinese people buy houses they often end up with the most neglected garden in their street, which can cause 'loss of face' in front of their friends and neighbours.

Negotiating in a Western Environment

Example Four
Enacting Strategy Seventeen

Strategy Seventeen can be applied in a Western business environment to motivate employees in order to improve their work productivity and performance. This is done by using Strategy Seventeen to present the *'the illusion of wealth'*, which can include bonuses. Employers can do this by using incentives to promote a particular behaviour or performance they believe is necessary for the organisation's success. The employee is given an amount of the company's annual profit to encourage the employee to work extra hard in achieving the future business goals.

By sacrificing a small amount of profit, an employer can in return gain something of much more value for the future growth of the company.

Key Points when using Strategy Seventeen

- Research your contacts well to find out what they value. What may be of relatively little value to you may be highly attractive to them.
- A small cost in the short term can produce much larger gains in the long term.
- The bait you use may not be financial, and could include giving someone 'face', which is very important for Chinese people.

To catch the bandits, first capture their leader *means "deal with the leader and their followers will do what you want"*

If the enemy's army is strong but is allied to the commander only by money or threats, then take aim at the leader. If the commander falls the rest of the army will disperse or come over to your side. If, however, they are allied to the leader through loyalty, then beware. The army can continue to fight on after his death out of vengeance.

*I*n 756 BC Commander Yin Ziqi besieged the city of Suiyang. Zhang Xun was the defending commander of Suiyang, and he noticed that Yin Ziqi stayed a long way from the battle and observed the action from a distance. In battles, Yin Ziqi had the reputation of letting his army do all of the work while making sure he saved himself. Although Yin Ziqi's army were strong fighters, they were only loyal to him because he would threaten to punish them with hard physical labour if they did not fight well. *'Yin Ziqi's army was strong but were allied to their commander by threats.'* Zhang Xun wanted to get closer to Yin Ziqi because he knew Yin Ziqi was not an experienced fighter. Zhang Xun devised a strategic plan for his expert archers to get close to Yin Ziqi.

Zhang Xun did this by applying Strategy Eighteen – **To catch the bandits, first capture their leader** to work, Zhang Xun knew '*if the commander falls the rest of the army will disperse*.' Yin Ziqi's army were only loyal to him as a result of the threats he made, so once Zhang Xun's army was able to capture Yin Ziqi, his army would not fight on. Instead, they would quickly retreat from the city of Suiyang. When Strategy Eighteen was successfully applied, Yin Ziqi's '*army would not continue to fight on after his death out of vengeance*.'

The next time Yin Ziqi's army attacked the walls of Suiyang, Zhang Xun ordered his army to shoot them with twigs instead of arrows. When Yin Ziqi observed they were firing twigs instead of arrows he was pleased, because it appeared that Zhang Xun's soldiers were running out of arrows. Once he observed this he moved closer to Suiyang to inspect the situation. As Yin Ziqi rode his horse closer to the town of Suiyang, he was surprised that he came into the range of Zhang Xun's archers who '*took aim at him.*' They had been saving their arrows for this moment. Zhang Xun's archers were in close range and fired an arrow into Yin Ziqi's eye. Unable to see, he fell off his horse, struck his head on a rock and died. As Yin Ziqi had continually treated his troops with threats, they were not prepared to continue to fight because he had not been a well-respected leader. On witnessing the death of their leader they swiftly left the battle grounds and Suiyang remained under the command of Zhang Xun.

When Strategy Eighteen is used, the strategist will attempt to remove the opposing leader, thus altering the motivations of their followers. The strategist must research the leadership style of their opposition, because Strategy Eighteen can only be successfully applied if loyalty towards the opposition leader is driven simply by money or threats.

Negotiating with Chinese People

EXAMPLE ONE
Strategy Eighteen in action (against you)

When deciding to conduct business in China, it is necessary to set aside a considerable amount of time in order to visit China on a regular basis. These visits are part of the recipe to build *guanxi*. It is calculated that a Western business person in the early stages of a new business venture needs to spend at least one week every two months in China. One scenario may be that you are a Western business person who has a business in the agricultural sector, and plan to export your high-quality beef to China. In your country you have a large property that produces beef, and you employ a team of thirty staff. Your first entry into the China market is through a trade show where you exhibit your products. At this trade show you meet a good Chinese contact and after several meetings you decide they are a reputable importer for your beef. They have good connections into the retail outlets, but you realise they will need some assistance in the marketing of your beef. You perceive this will work well, as you believe you have a strong team who are competent to manage the business when you are in China. Your leadership style is one that guides the business decisions on a daily basis as you are mostly on site every day.

To continue to develop *guanxi* you invite your contacts to your farm so they can see everything in operation and feel confident they are purchasing a reputable, high-quality product. They see that your style of leadership is one where you are involved in the day-to-day operations of the farm. To apply Strategy Eighteen, your Chinese contacts analyse your leadership style and conclude that without you in the business every day the business will not run as efficiently. As a result, your Chinese contacts perceive that eventually your business will develop internal project management and communication problems.

By recommending that you visit China every two months they are *'taking aim at the leader'*. The overall plan is that the rest of the workers on the farm will *'come over to them'* because they eventually plan to buy the business, which means the staff will become their employees. You visit China every two months, and because you are relatively new to China, you do not realise that it is not just the week you are in China, because in reality you need to spend a week prior to your trip in preparation and a week following your return to your own company to follow up your visit. Business people who are new to the China market often do not realise that travelling consumes a lot of time and energy, and it is difficult to continue to run the business in your own country. So, after one year of travelling to China you discover your farm in your own country is not operating as you would like it to. Your staff are not doing things as well as they did when you were guiding them. Your Chinese contacts require a lot of your time to assist with product displays in retail outlets, and this requirement of your time is part of the application of Strategy Eighteen. As Strategy Eighteen has been applied, your Chinese contacts watch and see the decline in your organisational structure. Even though your China export business is going well, the staff on your farm do not have the leadership they are accustomed to, and your domestic market then struggles to make a profit. This situation causes stress and your Chinese contacts offer to buy the whole business. To get out of this situation you accept a rather low price.

EXAMPLE ONE
Guarding yourself against Strategy Eighteen

An excellent way of guarding yourself against Strategy Eighteen is to be fully aware of your leadership style. If your leadership style is more about focusing on the day-to-day operations of your business, and you need to spend time visiting China at regular intervals in order to develop your business in China, it is likely your business will not be as productive as if you were physically there. Inevitably, this will create a weak link between you and your team. You may also want to question your Chinese contact's request for you to be in China every two months, as every three or four months may be adequate. You need to research and work out the time frame that is really needed. Succumbing to what your Chinese buyers want you to do is not good for the business relationship, because this behaviour merely displays your limited knowledge of China.

To guard yourself against the application of Strategy Eighteen it would be more beneficial to appoint a competent member of your team as your export manager. The first visit can be you, as it is important that the owner of the company develops the *guanxi*, but on the following visit you can take your export manager to introduce them to the China business. The following visits can then be handled by your export manager. If there are any important meetings to attend then you can agree to go to China. However, this would only be if it is really necessary for you to be there. In this way you will hand the China area of your business on to a staff member whose job it is to develop the China business, and you will not have to concentrate on both your export and domestic market that are geographically in two locations. It is crucial that your export manager understands how to conduct business in China, and in particular how the 36 Strategies are applied. By keeping your business solid in your own country and showing a strong leadership style where you are well respected amongst your team, you will leave no gaps for Strategy Eighteen to be applied on you by Chinese buyers.

Example Two
Strategy Eighteen in action (against you)

A key difference between how the Chinese business structure operates compared to the Western business structure is that the Chinese business environment is operated within a hierarchical framework, whereas a Western business structure operates within an egalitarian structure. This hierarchical framework has been discussed in Strategy Three – **Murder with a borrowed knife** which is in Book One – *Tame the tiger: Negotiating from a position of power.* When you visit China and are taken out to a restaurant it is likely you will observe this hierarchical structure at the banquet table. This is evident in the particular seating arrangement, and also in who is delegated to pay the bill. As discussed in Strategy Three, the highest-ranking person does very little. This behaviour displays that they are in control of the group. To see this hierarchical structure in action you may observe a simple head nod to the person who is allocated to pay the bill.

In a scenario where a Chinese delegation visits a Western country, the Western company who are hosting will be likely to operate in their own egalitarian structure. This structure allows your Chinese contacts to talk with all members of your group quite freely. As this is not organised as a strict hierarchal structure, you may be placed in a vulnerable position for Strategy Eighteen to be applied on you.

A scenario may be that you are an engineering company who has developed some highly sought-after intellectual property that your visiting Chinese contacts are interested in purchasing. You host a dinner for your Chinese contacts, and four of your most senior engineers attend. You do this for 'face', because you want to impress your Chinese contacts in order to convince them that you are the best company to deal with. In your company's leadership structure you have no boundaries between your status and that of your staff. At the dinner your staff and the Chinese delegates talk together with no visible hierarchy in place. Business cards are exchanged between the Chinese delegates and your team, and everyone is friendly.

The Chinese group perceives this as an opportunity to apply Strategy Eighteen by *'taking aim at the leader'*. They plan this by taking you out the next day after the dinner and talking with you about your team. During this meeting they find out the strengths and weaknesses of your engineers. After you meet with the group, you presume they are interested in buying your intellectual property. However, they contact each of your engineers independently. After discussing the details of a deal with each engineer they choose two of the engineers and offer them a deal directly without your involvement. In this case they were able to apply Strategy Eighteen to encourage your team *'to decide to come over to their side'*. The result is that you are cut out of the deal, as they have gone directly to your engineers.

EXAMPLE TWO
Guarding yourself against Strategy Eighteen

To guard yourself against Strategy Eighteen being successfully applied to you, and therefore preventing your Chinese contacts from going directly to your senior engineers to access your intellectual property, it is crucial that you operate in a hierarchical manner, even though your Western default is to work in a flatter structure. When you are meeting and dining with Chinese buyers in your own Western country, it will be beneficial to put a hierarchical structure in place. This hierarchical framework needs to display the status of the senior engineers in your company. From a Chinese point of view this status shows strong leadership. The best way to guard yourself against Strategy Eighteen is to have a strong leadership with a hierarchical structure in place. If you demonstrate that you are able to talk with anyone in your company and that there are few boundaries between people, this gives the Chinese contacts an opportunity to bring your senior engineers over to their side. If you do not put these boundaries in place, your Chinese contacts will use their expert negotiating skills, and it will not be difficult for them to contact your senior engineers independently and offer them a deal they will find difficult to refuse.

Key Points when Strategy Eighteen is used against you

- Be aware of your leadership style and consider how this structure may protect you or create vulnerability.
- Do not allow your Chinese business negotiations to damage your relationships with your team or cause you to neglect your leadership duties.
- If your Chinese business negotiations are interfering with your usual leadership duties, appoint a manager to operate the China side of your business.

EXAMPLE THREE
Enacting Strategy Eighteen

When you are planning to start, or are already, conducting business in the Greater China Region, it is a good idea to join an association in your own Western country that focuses on the Greater China Region. These associations may be Chambers of Commerce or other such organisations that can assist you to network with other people who are conducting business in the Greater China Region. These types of associations often have guest speakers who are experts in the region, and who can provide you with up-to-date information about China. They may also escort delegations to China or host visiting Chinese delegations. As these organisations deal specifically with the Greater China Region their president is often a Chinese person who has strong *guanxi*. It is likely that most of the committee members in the association are also Chinese. These organisations are no different to any other Chinese business structure, which means they operate in the usual hierarchical manner.

To apply Strategy Eighteen, you create a solid relationship with the leader of the organisation. If the leader wants to assist you with any China queries, then the committee members will follow. Therefore, to apply Strategy Eighteen, you *take aim at the leader'*. In this situation this means you will get close to the leader, and then the committee members will follow and *'come over to your side'* to offer you support

A likely scenario may be that your business has just commenced working with a company in China, and you have some documents that need translating. You have never done this before and have no idea where to start. You are aware that the association you belong to would be able to help you, but you are just one of 250 members and you know that simply calling their office will not be enough to get you the help you need. To apply Strategy Eighteen, you need to establish a relationship with the president by first introducing yourself at a function, then in that conversation inviting the president to your office. When they arrive at your office you mention you have no idea about translating and need some documents translated. As the president is in your office, it is highly likely they will want to offer assistance in order to gain 'face', and they will delegate this task to one of the committee members. In this situation *guanxi* has been developed between you and the president of the association, therefore the committee members will be obligated to follow the president's wishes. By applying Strategy Eighteen when you are a member of a Chinese association in your own Western country, you will achieve substantial benefits from your membership.

Negotiating in a Western Environment

EXAMPLE FOUR
Enacting Strategy Eighteen

Strategy Eighteen can be used in a Western environment when a situation arises where your company needs to recruit a new general manager. Traditional approaches would be to post an advertisement, conduct interviews with the likely candidates, and then select the best candidate. While this is a reasonable approach there is a risk, because you do not know if the person you have selected will actually be able to perform the required tasks. A general manager's position is a crucial position in an organisation, and therefore underperformance can be extremely detrimental to the company. To use Strategy Eighteen, you need to research several organisations that are similar to your company, and find out who their general managers are, and how successful they have been in this position. In this way you will know exactly what they are capable of. You will also know of the innovations of general managers who lead similar companies to yours who are actually your competitors.

To apply Strategy Eighteen, and therefore locate the most appropriate general manager for your business, you *'take aim at the leader'* by approaching the general manager who you would like to work in your company and offering a package, which is more than they are already receiving. This package is not merely driven by money, because it also includes several incentives, and you know from your research that these initiatives do not exist in the company they are currently working for. When Strategy Eighteen is applied *'they come over to your side'*, which means the general manager comes over to your company. Their methodology will come with them, and you will have successes similar to the success your competitors have enjoyed.

Key Points when using Strategy Eighteen

- Search for leaders with loyal followers.
- Make use of your Chinese associations in your own country and develop *guanxi* with the president of the Chinese Association to achieve the most out of your membership.
- Do not spread yourself too thinly by trying to develop too many relationships. Instead, focus your efforts on developing *guanxi* with the leader.

Your Next Steps

Having just finished reading *Lure the Tiger*, here are some suggestions for your next steps:

- Now I can plan my approach when I am negotiating in any situation.
- The 36 Strategies will help me when communicating with Chinese people.
- I will share this knowledge with my colleagues.
- I want to read *The Dao of Negotiation* series. I'll find them at **www.leoniemckeon.com**
- I will contact Leonie to:
  - Help me think completely differently about my business development challenges.
  - Deliver a presentation for my next conference or other event.
  - Deliver 36 Strategies workshops to my team.
- Because **Pronounce Mandarin - The Easy Way** is perfect for beginners, I will learn how to correctly pronounce Chinese names and some useful Mandarin Chinese words and phrases via **www.pronouncemandarin.com**

Go to **www.leoniemckeon.com** for more information about the 36 Strategies. Leonie has several informative videos and blogs to help you further your understanding of how to negotiate in any business environment.

WHAT PEOPLE SAY ABOUT WORKING WITH LEONIE MCKEON

BEC HARDY WINES

"I can't tell you how much you have given our family, and me personally, through your insights about the 36 Chinese Strategies. Understanding how the 36 Chinese Strategies are applied in Chinese business culture was the lightbulb moment which has led to such revenue growth, opportunities and personal growth. This has been one of the great, exciting professional and personal journeys and achievements of my life. Thanks again."

Richard Dolan, Joint Managing Director

HATCH, Western Australia

"Anyone who has the pleasure of having dealings with China and the Chinese will find Leonie's 36 Chinese Strategies workshops invaluable. The workshops were eye-opening and had the right amount of humour and personal stories to more than keep our attention."

Denis Pesci, PDG Hub Director, Western Australia

Fletcher Building

"From a personal perspective, Leonie was instrumental to our Chinese cultural program developed for the Super Retail Group. The target audience for the workshop was our Management and Leaders from Logistics, Marketing and Category. In organising the program for the team, I found Leonie incredibly resourceful, totally understood the brief and built value-add to the program. Often you don't know what you don't know so great to have a Subject Matter Expert to guide and shape a very successful program."

Shirley Brown, Capability Development Manager – Australian Distribution

Australian American Fulbright Commission

"The Art of Negotiation – 36 Strategies derived from 'The Art of War' workshop delivered by Leonie at the Australian Institute of Company Directors (AICD) challenged conventional thinking."

Peter de Cure, Chairman, Australian American Fulbright Commission

Kmart

"The training that Leonie provided to our team was excellent. The program was practical, delivered with context, and opened the team members' minds to learning more about how to do better business in China. I have no doubt that what we have learned will be applied and will provide great outcomes for our business. Leonie has also provided a great personal development opportunity for members of our team."

Matthew Webber, International Supply Chain Manager

The Dao of Negotiation
The Path between Eastern Strategies and Western Minds

		Strategy Number
Book One – *Tame the Tiger*	Advantageous Strategies	1, 2, 3, 4, 5, 6
Book Two – *Deceive the Dragon*	Opportunistic Strategies	7, 8, 9, 10, 11, 12,
Book Three – *Lure the Tiger*	Strategies for Attack	13, 14, 15, 16, 17, 18
Book Four – *Bewilder the Dragon*	Confusion Strategies	19, 20, 21, 22, 23, 24
Book Five – *Endure the Tiger*	Strategies for Gaining Ground	25, 26, 27, 28, 29, 30
Book Six – *Flee the Dragon*	Strategies for Desperate Situations	31, 32, 33, 34, 35, 36

The Dao of Negotiation:
The Path between Eastern Strategies and Western Minds

by Leonie McKeon

More Control, More Success, More Wins!

Based on *The Art of War*, *The Dao of Negotiation* series unmask the 36 Strategies used in Chinese culture and business.

This incredible series of 6 books provide invaluable tips for any business person looking to improve their overall negotiation skills, as well as become better at negotiating with Chinese People.

Discover how you can use this ancient wisdom for more business success.

www.leoniemckeon.com

www.ingramcontent.com/pod-product-compliance
Lightning Source LLC
Chambersburg PA
CBHW050608210326
41521CB00008B/1158